19

Remarkable

Northwest Women

19
REMARKABLE
NORTHWEST WOMEN

WHAT ARE THEY DOING NOW!

CAROLYN LEEPER

To the many wonderful women who
have befriended and mentored me
throughout the years.
Thank you!

Meet Wine Diva Deb, Captain Anne, P.I. Pam, and the rest of these 19 Remarkable Women.

CONTENTS

FOREWORD

Women's roles and responsibilities have seemed to be more of a habit or a cultural dictum than a practical playbook for creating and sustaining a healthy well-balanced lifestyle for work-life.

This is where Carolyn Leeper's work becomes relevant to all of us. It's about recognizing our emerging talents, honoring our individuality within the collective, using common sense, flexibility and commitment to make the positive changes necessary to create a lifestyle that feels right, supports our wildest imaginings and encourages us to reveal our authenticity.

Northwest Women introduces a group of brilliant and courageous women, role models from all walks of life, who are changing how people perceive themselves as they strive to create individual solutions and find their place in a world of increasing demands imposed by voluminous technological

1

advancements and a diverse global community. In this book, Carolyn Leeper skillfully points out: Attitude is everything!

As a psychotherapist, I recognized some common themes weaving throughout the stories given in Northwest Women. All of them stem from a well-developed awareness of how to evoke change through choice. It's this ability to make deliberate decisions and take decisive actions that provide the potential to create whatever you desire. Here are some real jewels:

• It is important to recognize the complex effects of your own consciousness. Conceptually, this means that 'what you think' directly affects your overall well-being and the way you live your life.

• The multiplicities of these effects contribute significantly to how you define yourself and what you believe you can accomplish. At any given moment, in any circumstance, your attitude is your belief system in action.

• What you think becomes the target you focus on. Your thoughts are creating an outward expression of a belief system held within your subconscious mind. The outward expression is your present reality.

In other words, to create the career, relationships and lifestyle you desire--the reality you want and deserve--first, look inward at the beliefs you currently hold about yourself. Next, consider the beliefs of the people whose opinions you value. Then review your attitude toward the world you live in.

Is there a belief system that stands in the way of making a change? Have you found an old habit anchored in a judgment made long ago that is no longer useful or relevant to your next business venture, career or a relationship? If so, you've just discovered the pathway to a new life and all it offers. The temporary obstacles have been those obsolete patterns of thinking that no longer represent you, your dreams, and your goals. The key: When you update your belief systems, you rewrite your life script. An easy-to-remember algorithm is: Beliefs create values, and values drive behaviors. If you think you can, you will. If you think you can't. . . . You know the answer.

To create a lifestyle that upholds our highest aspirations, illustrates with efficacy our limitless potential, reveals our innate knowledge and wisdom, and fully expresses our heart's passions and compassion is a universal vision shared by people everywhere. It is a sacred vow embedded deep within--we are born with it!

Then, seemingly, life happens. As adults, we say, reality sets in. My grandmother's favorite saying when she would not accept my answer to her serious question: Fiddlesticks! She didn't believe a word I said when I gave her my heart-felt belief about something. She was not going to accept that outcome as the one cast in stone. There would have to be a different answer. She would accept nothing less!

This dear ancestor was 4' 10" tall; bore 10 children, raising 9 to adulthood; was widowed in the spring when the eldest was 17 and the youngest was an infant. In the fall, foreclosure on the family farm brought a second finale, so with no place else to go, she packed all that was left: 9 children, 2 cows to pull the wagon, 1 horse and some chickens. To be near her remaining family, 2 brothers, she decided to walk across the Cascade Mountains. It was early October.

The trek from Coulee City (eastern Washington) to Arlington (west side, Snohomish County) took 2-plus months, I'm told, and is approximately 195 miles. The photo taken on the day she left – all packed and ready to go – is heart-shaking!

My reaction when I saw it was: Why attempt such a feat? No help available. Probably snow in the high country, and the pass. What was she thinking?

Her faith was strong, her belief in her ability to create a better life for herself and her family, even under those dire circumstances, was firm and steadfast. To take the next arduous step, she focused on the desired outcome--her new reality!

Moral to the story? If you want to make positive personal or professional life changes, look within. Self-empowerment starts with recognizing and fully realizing the resources we already possess.

Want something beautiful, loving, safe, fulfilling, in your life? Then deliberately develop the belief systems that will support you in your quest.

That's what the women in Northwest Women do. Notice as you read their stories how subliminally they evoked their own shift in perception to create their desired realities.

There is always more than one answer or one outcome. As grandmother would say, "Accept nothing less!"

Billie Miller
Psychotherapist, Author

INTRODUCTION

Women across the nation are choosing the types of jobs and career paths that they want, regardless of past traditions or restrictions. Women are CEOs of Fortune 500 companies. They are doctors, lawyers, judges, university professors, astronauts, scientists, writers, actors, movie directors and producers, professional athletes, accountants and coaches. They are entrepreneurs, creating and operating their own businesses. They are ambassadors, politicians and philanthropists. Currently, five states have women governors and more than half of the states have had women governors: Arizona has had five and Washington has had two. There are twenty women senators. Currently, both senators from California and both from Washington State are women.

What happens as women take on more and more career responsibilities outside the home?

In the introduction to her book, Women, Work & the Art of Savoir Faire, Author Mireille Guiliano says, "A sweeping 'women's issue' is achieving a healthy balance of work life with 'life' life." She asks, "What is the point of being a successful businesswoman if you are not happy?" She says, "We don't work in a vacuum. Our work is a part of the rest of our lives."

What is "work-life balance?" It isn't as simple as spending half of one's time at work and half at home. The balance has to be more flexible--some days or weeks focused on work, if that's what is needed, setting aside time-off for family and personal life. Depending on the job or her own circumstances, a woman might spend long hours working without any conflict at all. If she, for instance, is a realtor, she might spend many Sunday afternoons holding open house, keeping her schedule open to attend her children's afternoon soccer games or piano recitals.

Can a woman have it all? Can she achieve a work-life balance that actually works? The answer is a resounding, "Yes, she can." But she can't do it alone. She needs friends, supporters, networking groups, and family. Here are just a few of the many remarkable Northwest Women: creative, educated, professionally successful, community minded and socially active, who have figured out how to do this.

These women have found their place and are passionate about what they are doing. Their advice to young women today is to follow your passion, take your careers seriously, carefully consider what it is you want to accomplish, never give up, and help each other along the way.

They suggest that you should not be afraid to change directions if you are not happy in what you are doing, that your skills and talents will not be lost; they will continue to work for you wherever your passions carry you, just as they are all doing.

The profile sketches in this book are not to be considered biographical. These remarkable women have generously shared their personal stories, thoughts, and bits of advice, along with some hard times and some good times. Cheers to the good times!

ROBIN AKKERMAN

Robin Akkerman has had thirty-four years of a varied professional career, where twenty years have been hospitality industry related. She has served as the State Recording Secretary for Business & Professional Women (BPW/USA) of Washington State, and has five additional years in a State Chair position for BPW. Robin is a Parliamentarian and served two years as President of the EastSide Parliamentary Law Group, and two years as the State organization's secretary. Her industry affiliations include thirteen years with Meeting Professionals International (MPI) where she served two years on the MPI Board as the VP of Administration. Born and raised in Wisconsin, Robin and her husband made their way to the Seattle area in 1994. Currently, as Associate Director of Sales, she is in her thirteenth year at Willows Lodge in Woodinville, a luxury hotel and spa in the Woodinville Wine Country. Robin has been an active member of the Woodinville Chamber of Commerce during those thirteen years, serving on the Chamber Board for six years.

The Willows Lodge hosts weekend getaways, retreats, corporate meetings, conferences, and other special events. Robin likes the diversity of her job, being able to travel, and being the face of the Willows. She feels personal responsibility to her position, to the Willows and the people who work there. She reaches out to sister properties in Seattle, referring business to them when appropriate, and often receives referrals in return. Robin is always ready to take the extra step to reach her goals.

One extraordinary example of taking that extra step and reaching out to offer exceptional experiences to the community, four friends got together in April 2004 to form a women's wine education group. Their premise was that since women are the major wine purchasers, it was important to further wine knowledge to assist in this buying power. These four friends were: Robin Akkerman, Anne Alberg, Holly Leuning of Columbia Winery, and Tina Maloney, Chateau Ste Michelle Winery. They declared themselves "Divas" and formed Woodinville Women & Wine, dedicated to creating monthly events for women that "celebrate the friendship of women with wine and wine education." The focus was educating women about Woodinville Wine Country wines and lifestyle, with wine tasting, wine education, and networking opportunities at a variety of Woodinville Wine Country venues including wineries, lodges, and historical sites.

Their first event was held at the Willows Lodge in September. Each event was sold out and the women couldn't wait to sign up for the next one. Event offerings included food and wine pairings, barrel tastings, Wine 101, learning how to be a wine judge, panels with winemakers and vineyard owners, a Bastille Day picnic, sipping and shopping at winery gift shops, a summer solstice event, and winemaker dinners. The events continued for four years.

Robin's advice to young women is: Don't hesitate to ask questions such as: How can I help you? How did you get your job? How can I learn more? Don't just sit back and look for "what's in it for me?" Be involved.

Robin's birthday is June 9. Her horoscope chart indicates that she possesses personal power, charisma, and determination. She is sensitive and considerate, with a magnetic personality and a flair for the dramatic. For leisure activities, Robin still enjoys learning about wine, loves concerts, music, and the Green Bay Packers. See www.willowslodge.com.

ANNE ALBERG

Captain Anne Alberg was born into an entrepreneurial family. One of her first successful business endeavors was selling Alberg Cherries. "I was the first person to sell cherries on the side of the road in Seattle in the summer of 1979," Anne says with pride. As Editor of the Ballard High School yearbook, Anne hired her friends to distribute cherries directly to the consumer. When Mount St. Helens erupted in 1980, she offered free ash to get people to stop and buy the cherries. Always the risk taker, Anne spent 30 years working for various startup companies when she found a product or service she believed in. Throughout her career, Anne found herself sharing her wealth of knowledge with other entrepreneurs. With her brain always churning, Anne calls herself the "Idea Diva." In 2004, she and three friends founded Woodinville Women and Wine to help women learn about wine and to help wineries get exposure. This earned her the title of "Wine Diva."

Sailing has always been part of Anne's world. As a high school graduation present, her father gifted her sailing lessons with Windworks at Shilshole Marina. She went on to graduate from the University of Washington with a business degree in marketing and an emphasis on Entrepreneurship and International Business. Over the years, Anne developed a diverse business background which luckily included extensive international travel. She used her dynamic people skills learned from Dale Carnegie's How to Win Friends and Influence People to make many friends along life's journey. One of her favorite quotes is by Zig Ziglar: "You will get all you want in life if you help enough other people get what they want." Anne has served in leadership roles in many organizations such as the Medical Marketing Association, Woodinville Women and Wine, Seraph Capital, Neptune Sailing Club, and Snoqualmie Pass Planning Advisory Council. The Washington Business & Professional Women (BPW/WA) recognized Anne as their Young Careerist Award, as well as the Helen Thayer Woman of the Year Award. In addition to her leadership role, she earned the title of "Networking Diva" by teaching networking skills, mentoring others, and bringing in many new members herself.

Captain Anne developed her deep-rooted passion for sailing at an early age while crewing on a 34' Cal sailboat owned by her brother and his family. However, her dream of sailing the oceans of the world began in the fourth grade at North Beach Elementary in Ballard when two friends, Arne and Kristen, said their parents were taking them out of school to go sailing. She thought "Someday that is what I am going to do!" In 1987, her first international sailing vacation began with friends in St Maarten on a 40' Endeavor named "Good Fortune." A couple she meet along the way told her she belonged as a Charter Captain in the Caribbean. Anne brushed off the idea, as she was busy selling medical equipment to customers around the world. The thought of living the sailing lifestyle was always in the back of her mind. But from 1989-2001, Anne worked as the delivery skipper taking care of her brother's Beneteau 456. She took many friends and clients from around the world out sailing in Puget Sound.

Anne's global sailing adventures include the Leeward Islands in the Caribbean, Thailand, Myanmar, Australia, Belize, Palau, Mexico, British Virgin Islands, and the Inside Passage in Northern British Columbia.

In 2009, Anne decided it was finally time to turn that passion into a career. Captain Anne now has her USCG Six Pack Captain's License, her American Sailing Association Instructor Credentials, and a career that is a lifetime in the making. In addition to being a Charter Captain and a Sailing Instructor, Anne enjoys being a Delivery Skipper. She did an offshore delivery from Neah Bay to San Francisco in June 2013 and from San Francisco to San Diego in December 2013. A natural born teacher, she loves working with students to advance their sailing abilities to the next level. Captain Anne takes her students and charter guests on amazing sailing adventures both here in the Pacific Northwest and around the world. Here's a quote from one of her students: "Skipper Anne is strong, smart, hard-working, capable and seasoned. She is a patient, calm teacher, who is both knowledgeable and inspirational! Anne is truly a joy to sail with!"

Where does Captain Anne get her inspiration? Anne says, "One of my favorite moments is when I see the 'AHA' expression on my student's face. Some start off looking like deer in headlights, but all end up with great big smiles at the end of a day on the water. Anne hears many clients who are around fifty years old say I have always wanted to learn to sail, or, I used to sail with my dad when I was a child. It gives Anne great pleasure to be the one who gets to share time out on the water with each of them. "I know in my heart this is what I came on the earth to do and I will have no need to ever officially 'retire.'

Every experience and job I have ever had has brought me to this moment in time," Captain Anne says with a smile.

Anne's motto for living her life is great advice to women of all ages: Grow. Be inspired. Go after your dreams. Get involved in the leadership of an organization or in your community. Take continuing education classes. Write down your goals and review them on a regular basis. She says, "Amazing things happened during the first 50 years of my life. Now with wisdom from my lifetime of experiences, I am excited to see what I can create in the next 50 years!"

If you want to relax and enjoy the scenery, learn to sail, learn about the local waters, or give your spouse and children an adventure, Captain Anne's friendly personable nature makes her your perfect choice! See www.captainanne.com.

Anne's birthday is January 11. According to her horoscope she is a romantic, always searching for more from life than the obvious. She is hardworking, creative, and a perfectionist. She has a calming and patient aura in any situation.

ALMA ALEXANDER

Alma Alexander, when asked, "where are you from," tells us, "Hard question to answer. I was born in a country that doesn't exist on the world's maps any more, once-was-Yugoslavia. I grew up in various countries in Africa, got an education in England, lived in the Antipodes for a while, and then married into the United States. So where am I from? The answer to that depends a whole lot on the breadth and meaning of the question, and can be as dry and geographic or as broad and lyrical as you like."

She says she came to Bellingham because "The cedars called. I wanted a place I could return to after too many years of not having this, where I could look out the window and tell you what season we are in. This place does that for me beautifully."

Alma's family consists of herself, husband Deck, and a vocal tux queen cat named Laptop. "We lost her brother, Boboko, in the fall of 2012. He is much missed and I believe his loving spirit still haunts my house. A new addition to the family (he arrived the day before New Year's Eve) is a one-eyed ex-feral shelter adoptee who diligently fails to respond to the name Blackjack. He and the resident feline are still coming to terms as to hierarchical issues."

A successful and prolific writer of fantasy and science fiction, when Alma's asked how she became a writer, she says, "I didn't become anything. I always was. This was just something that was a part of myself for as long as I existed, and I wrote from a very young age. My first full novel was completed before I was 11. My first GOOD novel, by age 14. I was winning national writing awards while I was a teenager, publishing stuff by the time I was 19, going full-time in the new millennium."

Asked why she became a writer, her reply is much the same: "There is no why. This is a vocation. You may as well try and ask a believer precisely WHY they believe in their god. When you have the voices in your head you just listen, because there is no other choice. And there are voices in my head. I've heard this writing bug being called a form of benign possession and there's something to that. There is something inside of you that is called Story and it wants out. Your hands and your mind are the tools that it has to achieve this. So you write. It's not something you can ever quite explain."

With an MSc in Microbiology and Molecular Biology, Alma worked in a lab, briefly, she says. She fled sideways fairly quickly into scientific writing and editing, and into related fields, reviewing, etc. Writing was part of it all, though. She says, "The novel that became the "Changer of Days" duology was actually literally written while waiting for experiments to finish cooking in the lab, so you might say that everything else I've done has just been icing on the cake."

Alma says she enjoys reading, needlework, photography, travel, coffee, animals, snow, teddy bears, puns, friends, mountains, wolves, whales, stars, music, the occasional decent movie, and Van Gogh's Sunflowers. She says she enjoys reading anything well written, anything that will transport her into a different world that she can believe in as much as, if not more than, the one she lives in every day. "But if I get starved for that," she says, "I'll read cereal boxes and then make up stories from what I find out there."

For her goals right now, Alma says, "Living the kind of life which has something in it by which one will be remembered." She belongs to the Whatcom Writers and Publishers group (WWP), the Science Fiction Writers of America (SFWA), and the Mythopoeic Society.

Advice to young women today according to Alma would be, "Don't let anyone tell you that they know better than you what your lives should be. Stand tall, be strong, make your own choices, make your own dreams come true, live your own lives. Love deeply, laugh often, be passionate about things you care about, have opinions and defend them, and don't forget to rest your soul by lifting your eyes to the starry skies on a clear night in a place where no human lights mar the darkness around you. Remember that without that true darkness you cannot see the true light."

Alma's birthday is July 5. Her horoscope shows that she is excellent at business, having what many people think of as good luck because she is typically successful in whatever she sets out to do. She is accomplishment-oriented, tending to attract success with a powerful though quiet aura. To learn more about Alma, visit her website: www.AlmaAlexander.org.

PAMELA BEASON

Pamela Beason is a novelist, a technical writer, a private investigator, and an adventurer with a passion for hiking, kayaking, and scuba diving. She loves horseback riding. She paints, quilts, and does country line dancing. She says, "I'm always so frustrated that I'm only one person!"

Pam was born in the tiny town of Sedan, Kansas, and lived in Kansas, South Carolina, Ohio, and Oklahoma as well as in Washington State. She's lived the Pacific NW longer than anywhere else, though, since 1979.

She was a managing editor at Microsoft, but when she left there she decided she wanted to live in a less commercially-oriented area. She says, "I am a kayaker and a hiker and I'm fairly liberal politically, so Bellingham seemed a natural place for me. I always say that in Redmond, people live to work, and in Bellingham, people work to live (if they work at all). I love the way that people here talk about movies and books and life in general instead of discussing all the trivia of their work life."

Her mother lives in Redmond and she has a sister who lives in Owasso, Oklahoma. Her father and brother passed away a few years ago. "My extended family," Pam says, "is spread throughout Kansas and Oklahoma with a few of us more rebellious types up here in Oregon and Washington." She has two cats, "Lassie, a sweet placid calico, and Ruusky, an incorrigible but charismatic Russian Blue serial killer."

Pam says she actually became a private investigator because she realized that most of her freelance tech writing and editing work was being shipped overseas. She says, "Investigation work requires a lot of the same skills: doing research and interviews and writing unambiguous reports that will stand up under legal scrutiny. I just have to be more secretive and talk to a few more criminal types with investigation work."

As a private investigator, Pam likes the fact that she is always learning something new about different types of businesses, about different types of scams, about human nature. She says, "In investigation work, I talk to a lot more different people than I did in the technical writing world."

Pam has always been a writer but now she spends at least half of her working life writing fiction, which has always been her true love. She says, "I've done so many things, it's hard to remember: geologic research, mechanical and architectural drafting, translation work, tech writing and editing, managing multimedia and travel writing teams at Microsoft, teaching Spanish and writing skills in colleges, training employees to use various computer programs." In college she planted trees for the Forest Service, tutored vets in English and Spanish, did computer coding for the Federal Aviation Administration, and other odd jobs. She adds, "My eclectic work history helps a lot in my writing and investigation work. I know something about almost every type of field, so it's pretty hard to fool me. I was also the only student in my investigation course who knew how to draw a crime scene to scale. Every piece of knowledge and experience pays off in the long run."

Pam has a B.A. in Latin American Studies and an M.A. in Spanish but says her education is fairly irrelevant to her work. She explains, "I had interviews with the CIA a couple of times in my younger years and I've been better able to compete with other job seekers because of my languages, but other than that, those degrees have not impacted my life. If I'd been a gutsier, more sophisticated child, I would have studied a natural science of some kind, but my family lived in Oklahoma, I'd never met a scientist, and at that time, most scientific fields didn't seem open to women."

Calling herself an addict of the written word, Pam says, "I read everything that I find interesting: biographies, true adventures, good romances, science fiction, mysteries, you name it." The only categories she doesn't enjoy are lifestyles of the rich and famous, series romances, erotica, chick-lit type books that focus on shoes and clothes and shopping, and cozy mysteries that focus on cooking or other activities that are not personally interesting to her. She adds, "I'm dangerous in the kitchen. I often joke that I should write a cookbook called When the Smoke Alarm Goes Off, It's Done. On the positive side, I have learned to create all sorts of alternative building materials in my oven and microwave using only common household ingredients."

She is a member of a variety of organizations: The Sierra Club, WAKE (Whatcom Association of Kayak Enthusiasts, Mount Baker Club (outdoor club), Upstart Crows Writers Association, Romance Writers of America, Mystery Writers of

America, and Whatcom Writers & Publishers. Inspired by nature more than anything else, Pam asks, "How can anyone look at a waterfall, a field of wildflowers, an octopus, or a mountain lion and not think this is an incredible planet we live on?"

With such a varied background, Pam says that a lot of people know different things about her, so she likes to think that she often surprises nearly everyone but her family. Once when she was in Kenya she surprised her group by pushing aside the guide to change a tire on the Land Rover as a herd of Cape Buffalo closed around them. "I did that because I am one of the fastest tire changers you'll ever meet," she says, "due to the fact that I used to 'borrow' tires in college so I could pass the annual vehicle inspection." After that incident, she says, the guide ran around pointing to her and saying to all the other Africans, "This is a valuable woman." She likes to think she has surprised most everyone who knows her at least once. She says her life, though, is an open book, "just a really long unedited one." See www.pamelabeason.com

Her advice to young women today would be: "Be honest with yourself about what you like and don't like, find your own strengths, work hard and don't depend on others to make you happy or pay your bills, and never be afraid to change course if the path you're on isn't making you happy."

Pam's birthday is June 28. Her horoscope chart indicates that while she enjoys bouncing ideas off other people she ultimately makes her own choices and does her own thing. She is very perceptive and a natural leader and is expert at seeing both sides of a situation.

KATHRYN BROWN

Kathryn Brown has found her passion: helping new and talented writers become known to the readers of the world. Focused on the digital publishing phenomenon that is, she says, "changing the world of publishing like nothing since the invention of the moveable type printing press. Not long ago there were only about 300,000 new titles each year, now there were more than two million books published in the English language in 2013."

How do readers decide what to read? The traditional way is to browse through the book store and spend actual face time with the books, choosing a book by the appearance and appeal of the cover, perhaps the picture on the cover, the title, or by the author. With this method still very much in place, how does a new author with a self-published book, print or digital, reach the readers?

This is where Kathryn and her business, Chanticleer Book Reviews, comes in, providing social media coverage with book reviews, contests, comments, as well as bringing authors and readers together with Facebook, twitter, etc. The motto of Chanticleer Book Reviews & Media is: We Help Books Get Discovered in Today's Era of Unbounded Publishing.

As president of the Whatcom Writers and Publishers organization, in Bellingham, Kathryn associates closely with writers of all genres, talent, and level of experience.

Chanticleer, now heading into its fourth year, works with small independent book stores to highlight talented new authors by furnishing print copies of their books at no cost to the store, with the books setup in special promotional display areas. Kathryn speaks at writers conferences promoting the books as well as providing book reviews and contests. She also presents at writing conferences and conventions.

With an educational background in business management and marketing, Kathryn describes herself as a "serial entrepreneur," having run several different retail businesses. She is creative, even visionary, and understands the need to take risks in business, with her practical side keeping those risks under control. Another aspect of Kathryn's life is sailing, something she truly loves. She served for a time as Trustee of the Bellingham Yacht Club.

The daughter of a Marine Sergeant, Kathryn's growing up years involved moving from place to place, experiencing the differing lifestyles around the country but she considers herself a southerner, with well-bred southern manners and hospitality being a given. One of her goals is to travel more in the future, perhaps living a few months here and a few months there, always moving on to another fascinating place. Another goal is to finally do some writing herself. She says she has always had stories in her head but never had the time to write. Her first book would probably be something of an epic fantasy. Another might be about Norwegian Fairy Cats.

Kathryn's advice to young women today is a resounding, "Be open. Keep your eyes open for new opportunities." See www.chantireviews.com.

Born on September 4, Kathryn's horoscope chart indicates that she is goal oriented, resourceful, makes positive connections with others, and has the ability to concentrate on what really matters. Her domestic and career needs are not in competition with one another. Her inner needs tend to be mirrored by external events, and vice versa.

JALIMA COLLINS

Jalima Collins was already a successful young businesswoman in Nicaragua in the 1970s, operating a company that supplied mercantile products to the maritime industry there, when the country was engulfed in war and taken over by Communists. "I was so focused on my business, I didn't realize what communism meant," she says. Private business was nationalized. Both she and her husband were imprisoned but escaped and eventually arrived in Los Angeles.

Jalima immediately took to the possibilities she saw in this country. She went to college to learn English and quickly found work, but her husband could not adjust to America. He and Jalima divorced and he went back to Nicaragua. The divorce was devastating emotionally to her, but it came down to a life choice. "I could visualize a new, better life in America, and I had a lot of ambition. I did not want to go back and he did."

With her strong entrepreneurial spirit, Jalima began a cleaning service while studying to become an antique appraiser. When she received that certification she opened her own antique business and both businesses prospered. "Knowing how to care for antiques, rare art and other quality items enhanced my cleaning business," Jalima says. "I was able to recognize and give careful handling and special treatment to items that were part of high-end home décor."

While the events in Nicaragua may be a distant memory for her, the experience continues to influence how she operates a business and she doesn't take for granted the privileges that come with being in a society that allows open commerce. "What I learned," she says, "is that you have to be determined when it comes to trying to reach your goals. Circumstances can change quickly and your chance may disappear."

The dream of becoming a business owner was a difficult one for Jalima from the start. She had to go against the wishes of her family culture. The family originally came from Persia in an area that is now Iran. "My family had a very strong entrepreneurial background and I was helping in the family business since I was nine," she says, "but women were discouraged from actually owning a business. I was twenty-one and I didn't want to continue going to school. I wanted to show them that I could do it on my own." She presented a plan to save a failing store, took over the ownership, and in a few years turned it into a successful operation. Her family still did not approve. "My dad was so embarrassed that he wouldn't talk to me. It was years before I could step back into the family home. But he eventually accepted what I was doing and realized that I wasn't going to change, and our relationship improved." Today Jalima calls her family in Nicaragua once a week and travels to her hometown once a year.

Although returning to Nicaragua is not in her plans, she does recognize that the country has free elections and is rebuilding its economy, although she says it has a long way to go. "What has improved," she says, "is education. More people are going to school and everyone wants to be a doctor."

Jalima did remarry and when her husband retired from the motion picture industry they visited Bellingham and fell in love with it, moving here in 1995. She soon founded Professional Cleaning Services, specializing in high-end homes, and has been carefully expanding her business to include the commercial market; small offices, construction houses, and rentals that have been deemed unsalvageable. She explains, "We are licensed, bonded, and now insured for the commercial market, but we will continue to maintain our previous services. Being multi-faceted has always worked in my favor."

Asked what makes her services different, Jalima says, "We listen to you and clean your house the way you want it done, with attention to detail. We always do deep cleaning, every time, not just on the surface." Jalima stresses Consistency, Security, and Safety. "You will have the same housekeeper most of the time, and the day and time will generally be the same every month unless you request a change. Staff is thoroughly screened and most are long-term employees. They are carefully trained to work with your fragile possessions."

"I will meet with you personally, discuss what your needs are, and give you a firm estimate," Jamima says. Professional Cleaning Services charge by the job, not by the hour, and you don't have to sign a contract. She guarantees that you will be happy with their work.

Looking back at her life, Jalima says, "I have been at the bottom, left with nothing more that the clothes I stood in. I survived and pulled myself back up. Sometimes I hear people complaining about how difficult it is to get a job or start a business and I just shake my head. This is a great place to do business. Don't sit back, though, expecting everything to be handed to you." Her advice to young women today would be: "Work hard and follow the rules and you can succeed. I know."

Jalima's birthday is August 23. Her horoscope chart indicates a person with strong creativity, who believes in her dreams, with an idealistic streak. She is generous and warm-hearted, but may experience more than her share of ups and downs.

Nanette Davis

Nanette J. Davis, Ph.D, spent 15 years at Western Washington University in Bellingham, Washington. She received her Ph.D. from Michigan State University and completed her post-doctorate studies at Stanford University. With more than three decades of experience as a teacher, writer, advocate, researcher and lecturer, Nanette is a recognized authority on issues relating to women, families, youth, and older adults. Her scholarly work includes numerous print books, and more than 100 articles and research reports. She is active in numerous community organizations, and was recently selected President of the Western Washington University Retirement Association (WWURA).

In Youth Crisis, Nanette takes a comprehensive look at the social condition of youth in contemporary society. The book examines what it means to grow up today, and discusses childhood through the ages, schooling, gangs and the difficulties faced by homeless, addicted and minority youth. Youth Crisis goes on to suggest ways that we might transform our culture, even our world, so that the youth of tomorrow will fare better than those of today.

Drawing on her own personal experience as her husband's caregiver for four years, Nanette has given us three books for caregivers: Blessed is She... Elder Care: Women's Stories of Choice, Challenge and Commitment; Caregiving Our Loved Ones: Stories and Strategies That Will Change Your Life; and The ABCs of Caregiving: Words to Inspire You.

Nanette says that Blessed Is She draws its title from Psalm 41—"Blessed is she who has regard for the weak; the Lord delivers her in times of trouble"—which suggests the spiritual power available to elder caregivers who are caring for the weakest among us. What prompted her to write this book, she says, "are the host of women (and men, as well), who urged me to speak out on behalf of those sacrificing their lives and hopes. My aim was to raise the level of awareness about longevity and the aging process, which has inherent rewards, but also pains, that all families must address." Part scholarly analysis, part memoir, Blessed Is She has three distinctive parts, exploring not only the negative aspects of caregiving, which are carefully documented, but also its positive and life-affirming facets.

Caregiving Our Loved Ones: Stories and Strategies That Will Change Your Life features in-depth interviews with more than 60 women. She gives readers insight into their individual challenges and collective bravery. Her honest portrayals show just how overwhelming, yet rewarding, caregiving can be. She says, "I have chosen to introduce the book with my own narrative. I discovered that while every caregiver's story is hers alone, each echoes that of other caregivers. I also weave my story throughout the rest of the chapters to demonstrate my personal connection to caregiving. Here, I emphasize how the road I have traveled is like that of so many others. I am not alone."

Nanette's latest book, *The ABCs of Caregiving: Words to Inspire You*, provides down-to-earth, positive, practical advice on how caregiving a loved one can be accomplished with the caregiver still maintaining her own mental and spiritual stability. She stresses the need for support from family members and friends, in addition to taking personal time to reflect and relax.

As she continues to write and make appearances across the Pacific Northwest, Nanette emphasizes the gifts of caregiving and the importance of self-care. She reminds caregivers to both ask for and accept help and recognize their own vulnerabilities.

In her advice to young women today, Nanette says, "The reality for younger women is that career and family are huge juggling acts. Each career, homemaker, mother, and work outside the home demands your full-time attention. How to live when you're often split is something every woman with dual roles must learn. It requires intense discipline and profound commitment. If you get sidetracked or have career or family setbacks, you need to just saddle up again, and go forward. Even keeping a job, much less maintaining a career, gets to be heavy going while raising kids. Actually, I often spout out, jokingly, that I'd rather be in real estate, but the truth is, I had a very superb career that I wouldn't trade for anything."

Sticktuitiveness, one of my professors said, is the way to go. I might have had a harder time without a fully supportive husband who kept urging me on when I had those moments of terror or doubt. He wouldn't accept my stopping or interrupting my career when I felt that I've had enough of this double life-- and I want the peace, security and comfort of home life. Both of us were in the same profession (academe) and he knew the hazards of what happens to women who drop out because family life makes more demands than we can reasonably handle. I have to admit, he was very successful, ending up as Dean of Arts & Sciences at Western, and he often did MORE than his 50% share.

Retired now and happily married to former educator Burl Harmon, Nanette makes time to unwind and enjoy life. She and Burl vacation regularly in both Hawaii and Mexico. Community-minded, they perform music together for local seniors and are actively involved with Whatcom Writers and Publishers and the Western Washington University Retirement Association.

Nanette's daughter, Susan Colleen Browne, is a writer and creative writing instructor, while another daughter, Patricia, is a business writer and editor. Her other four children, Katherine, Elizabeth, Timothy and Michael, live around the Pacific Northwest, allowing for frequent family visits.

Born on June 1, Nanette's astrology chart shows she has a lightning quick mind and a unique wit. Her love of entertaining and her friendly nature make her a lively companion. Partnership is extremely important to her and she thrives with the support of a significant other.

SARA GEBALLE

Sara Geballe, with a Bachelor degree in Biology from Cornell University and a Masters degree in Genetics from the University of Washington, found her passion was not in research but rather in communication.

Spending a year in France when she was just 20 years old increased her interest in language and culture. As an award-winning journalist, she has worked as a science and medicine reporter, science editor, community newspaper editor, university publicist, features reporter, freelance writer, workshop presenter, and sign language interpreter.

Sara is a Nationally Certified Sign Language Interpreter and provides sign language interpreting services in various settings including: university/college, corporate, medical, social services, community, and workplace. She served as editor for the Deaf Community News in Boston, overseeing all aspects of publication for that community newspaper.

From 1996 to 2003 she owned Seattle Diversity Works, offering customized trainings and consulting services to several hundred Northwest businesses on how to integrate deaf/hard-of-hearing jobseekers into today's workforce. She developed a suite of manuals and instructional materials and provided a range of job development and placement services to job seekers with disabilities.

As a freelance writer, Sara was a regular contributor to the Whatcom Independent newspaper and the Northwest Business Monthly magazine, and received numerous awards from the Washington Press Association.

In what may be a natural progression in the art of communication, Sara enrolled in a yearlong class, Writing the Modern Memoir, at Western Washington University. In writing her own memoir, she saw the incredible power and personal benefit of putting down in words the stories of a lifetime, and sharing those tales with loved ones.

Sara is a member of the Association of Personal Historians and the owner of Memoir Crafters (www.MemoirCrafters. com). She is committed to helping others in creating their own life stories in written form. She works one-on-one with clients to assist them in turning their memories into beautifully designed memoir books which become important keepsakes for loved ones and future generations. With some individuals, she conducts a series of interviews where the client simply talks, telling Sara story after story of the events of his life. From those oral interviews, Sara creates a lively manuscript written in the first person.

Before working with memoir book clients, Sara provides each with a several page questionnaire to capture the basics such as: mother and father's names, children's names and ages, grandparents' names and dates, places lived, schools attended, work history, travel, hobbies, and other interests. Sara explains, "The questionnaire helps me prepare for the first interview session with a new client, and it also helps the client prepare by getting their facts all in a row."

Other clients have already written their stories and need an editor who can bring it all together. Sometimes people have hundreds of pages of memoir, but they have a difficult time figuring out what to include and what not to. Or, they don't know how to turn a massive amount of material into a book of reasonable length that flows and loved ones will want to read. Using her polished editor's eye, Sara assists clients in creating that overarching structure, separating the wheat from the chaff.

With all her book clients, once the manuscript is complete, Sara next works with them to help select their most cherished photographs and other visuals to further bring their stories to life. These visuals may include love letters, diary entries, family trees, original artwork, family recipes, award letters, birth certificates, or just about any historical artifact that can be scanned.

Sara also assists individuals in crafting their ethical wills or legacy letters – powerful documents which express a person's core values, beliefs, life lessons learned, and future wishes for family and loved ones. These are smaller projects than the complete memoirs, but if the client desires each legacy letter can be transformed into a small, custom-designed book by adding photographs and other treasured visuals.

In addition, Sara offers a variety of workshops and trainings on memoir writing. She poses questions to get participants to think back on their lives and trigger their memories. Writing prompts might include asking participants to recall a favorite room or place in their childhood home and start jotting down all the memories and impressions that are evoked by the recollections. Or, she might ask them to think about the first time they were allowed to go somewhere all alone and what that experience was like and how it felt. In the course of each workshop, attendees experience firsthand how one recollection naturally triggers another and another, the participants going deeper and deeper to retrieve forgotten memories and stories.

Sara points out that the memoir questionnaire she asks people to fill out before beginning work on their book is completely different from the types of prompts she conducts in the workshops. "The questionnaire is a way for me to gather the factual information on a person's life and saves a lot of time during the interview part. It is kind of a left brain function, whereas the workshop prompts are more creative, right brain activities," Sara says.

With a continuing love for France, Sara and her husband, Steve James, also enjoy travel and recently spent three weeks in Paris, doing a house-exchange through Intervac.com. She points out the win-win aspects of the home-exchange program. She says they have been doing this house-exchange for three years and have never had, or even heard of, any problems. They have even met and become friends with several of the families.

Sara has two grown children: a son, Zachary, and a daughter, Ruby. Considering her own life choices, she is very glad that she completed her education at a young age, before starting a family. She believes it is very hard for a woman to go back to school and raise a family at the same time.

Her advice to young women today would be to be open to opportunities, do what you love, don't stay in a job you hate just for the security of the paycheck. "And," she says, "the skills you develop in one job will go with you, they're never wasted."

When Sara is not working on clients' memoirs or busy serving as a sign language interpreter, she loves reading, walking, bicycle riding, traveling, and keeping up her French. She also is a big Seattle Mariners fan, even though the team has not fared well in recent years.

Sara's birthday is March 7. Her horoscope chart tells that she is a true artist at heart, with an unusual perspective on life, has a need to feel connected to something higher than herself, and to make a solid contribution to the world. She has a tremendous imagination and is a fanciful story teller.

CHIKEOLA KARIMOU

Chikeola Karimou's business card reads, "The Stellar C.E.O., Awakening the Greatness Within." She says, "I help people boldly step forward and claim their Stellar Life. I have been interested in the field of spirituality for over twenty-five years and am always passionate and excited about knowing more, understanding more and simplifying more. I have come to understand the practice of Awareness and how to apply it while in the mist of our daily activities, mundane or otherwise."

Chikeola grew up in Cote d'Ivoire, on the coast of West Africa and moved to New York about twenty years ago. She lived for eight years in Manhattan, a couple of years in Larchmont, upstate New York and then Greenwich, Connecticut. She worked at the United Nations as a Tour Guide, then went back to school and got a MA in Art Gallery Management from the Fashion Institute of Technology.

She chose to follow her spiritual path and get involved in the healing arts of yoga and Feng Shui. She is registered with Yoga Alliance at the experienced teacher level of ERYT 500 and she earned her Feng Shui certificate with the Hollis Institute in New York. About moving to Bellingham she says, "I was feeling an energy shift in me and felt it was time to go, and so here I am." She named her business Lifestyle Well-Being because, she says, "I am truly interested in people taking good care of themselves. I am a disciple of Yoga. After years of practice, observation and research, I also found that balancing and harmonizing the space we live and work in is also an integral part of our well-being, and that's where the Feng Shui comes in." Now Chikeola is focused on her new business, The Stellar C.E.O. She helps clients open up to new understanding of themselves, finding meaning in their lives, and teaches them how to translate that success into all areas for greater success and fulfillment.

Speaking of the Bellingham community, she says, "I simply love the beauty of the place...not that New York or Larchmont or Greenwich, Connecticut, for that matter, are not beautiful. It's a different kind of beauty. Here, the energy of mother nature is so powerful, it is palpable. I am a walker. I love going out and walking and that gives me the chance to really know the neighborhoods and admire people's beautiful gardens, the architecture of homes."

Chikeola's interests are wide and varied. Besides her native language, she is fluent in Spanish, French, and English. She loves art galleries, tennis, dancing, and Agatha Christie mysteries. And, she says, "Getting together with friends is a big part of my life." About plans for your future, Chikeola says she wants to continue assisting people as much as she can. Her advice to young women today would be to know yourself, open up your mind and emotions and understand who you really are, what you are seeking, what truly makes you happy. See www.thestellarceo.com.

Chikeola's birthday is September 20. Her horoscope chart indicates that she has a gentle, peaceable manner, that she is generally quiet and likeable, and has a strength of character that others sense. She seeks security and harmony in her life.

Maureen Kelly

Maureen Kelly is the author of WINE TYPES - Discover Your Inner Grape, a lighthearted approach to a serious subject: communication, exploring your own personality type through comparison with wine types. Are you a: Cabernet? A Champagne? A Pinot Noir? A Merlot? Maureen says you will enjoy this book if:

* You love to drink wine but aren't really concerned about the 'nose'
* You love to drink wine and are concerned about the 'nose'
* You love to drink wine and just want to learn more about YOU
* You don't even drink wine but want to learn more about YOU

Maureen became interested in personality types when she was introduced to the Myers Briggs Type Indicator. She was impressed by the instrument from the standpoint of learning about herself (realizing her strengths as well as her points of vulnerability) and the invaluable information the test shared regarding understanding the behavior of others in her life. She says it was a life-changing experience.

She began conducting MBTI workshops on the east coast with a mentor and then also for NW Airlines. She says, "I have branched out into many other areas because I very much enjoy teaching and sharing what means so much to me in my own life."

Maureen says she views writing as a way to express what she is feeling in her heart and soul. She say, "Writing is a medium to share what matters most to me in my life and also extremely 'cleansing' i.e., a way to fully integrate life experience and what it means to me."

One of her goals would be to open her own healing space to accommodate classes and workshops. Maureen is involved in healing practices: yoga, sound healing, and acupressure for both two and four-legged. In her second book PET TYPES: Communing Heart to Heart, she asks, "Do you and your pet have a lot in common?" You can learn more about how you and your 'furry kids' interact; discover how awareness of personality types can bring us closer and also inspire the humor in life and share in the philosophical conversations that form in a daily exchange of thoughts in "Dog Walk Talk." She says, "Seeing things from different perspectives can either cause a rift to form OR provide a foundation for growth." Maureen is an Ambassador for the Grey Muzzle Organization (senior dog rescue).

In ENERGY TYPES: Personality, Chakras & Balance, Maureen shows the connections between mind, body, and destiny. She says, "As we raise awareness regarding our inborn tendencies, we can then celebrate our strengths as well as monitor areas in our various energy fields where a proclivity for 'tipping the scales' may exist." She asks, "Would our time on this planet be different if we were handed an instruction manual upon our arrival? Welcome to Earth. Take a moment to read over the following guidelines to streamline and enhance your mortal experience and allow you to be the very best human being you can be."

In previous jobs, Maureen was an On Board Service Manager for NW Airlines, a Web designer, and currently is still a Yoga Instructor. She has a varied educational background: University of San Francisco (one year Nursing/ one year English); Friedrich-Alexander Universitat, Erlangen, Germany (German, French & Italian) two years; University of Maryland, Nuremberg, Germany (German–two years).

Maureen now lives in beautiful Birch Bay, Washington. She was born in Portland, Oregon, and raised in the San Francisco Bay area in California. After years of living in Europe and Washington, DC, and a period in Nashville, she wanted to return to the west coast. Her brother lives in Southern California. She has two dogs (one fourteen year old chow mix and one seven year old golden retriever) and two cats (one seventeen year old silver tabby and one six year old pure white deaf kitty).

She enjoys reading and intimate discussions with friends about life, taking her dogs to the meadows, meditation, sharing wine with friends, laughing. She particularly likes reading books on spirituality, healing novels that have an intriguing 'real' storyline, such as Kite Runner. What might surprise everyone is that she speaks fluent German and was a Bavarian Triathlon champion!

The advice Maureen would give young women today is to follow your heart and always be authentic. She is inspired by laughter and kindness. Asked what she would want people to know about her, she says, "Well I'm not exactly sure…maybe why I'm joyful most of the time?" See www.winetypes.net.

Maureen's birthday is February 14, Valentine's Day. She jokes that she "chose it." Her horoscope indicates that she is youthful at any age, spirited and playful, and yet a hard worker. She is a natural born entrepreneur with unique ideas.

Karla Locke

Karla Locke and her husband Tony suffered a devastating loss of their Seattle audio/video business in 2005. Wanting some place to quietly recover and get their lives back on track, they coasted into Anacortes thinking they would hang out for a year or two.

Karla says, "What neither of us expected was how much we would fall in love with this wonderful little community and the surrounding area. At the time, I wasn't sure how a big city girl would adjust to a small town. Well, adjust I did. After opening up That Photo Shoppe, I started organizing photography workshops and I became involved with the Skagit Valley Camera Club." She also belongs to the Skagit Valley Writers League and is on the Anacortes Arts Commission.

At first she had no real interest in taking up photography. "My talent and passion was in organizing workshops," she says.

"I teamed up with photographers and instructors, Dick Garvey, Vince Streano, and Tony Locke, and after years of watching, learning and absorbing, I was hooked and got my first camera. I am no longer a city girl. I love living in Anacortes." With Armchair ePublishing, Karla provides services to writers who want to self-publish.

Karla, a writer herself, is also an avid reader. She says, "A friend turned me on to romances when I was in my early twenties and I have been reading ever since. I also like thrillers and some paranormal romances. And once in a while I will venture outside the norm and read something that I would not normally read, for example: I just read, More Than You Know by Nan Rossiter. Not my usual reading but a very good book."

She plans to continue writing, even though her friends were surprised that she self-published her first story or that she was even trying to write. She wants to travel and meet people. Karla says she is inspired by people. Karla was born in Kimball, Nebraska and raised in Denver, Colorado. She has two sons and one daughter-in-law but no grandchildren.

What advice would Karla give young women today? She says, "Explore. Explore the world, yourself, life. Don't let the day-to-day stuff bog you down. I just wish I had spent more time seriously considering my career when I was in my twenties. Everyone has a talent, a passion, a way to express themselves; I express myself through organizing creative workshops or events for photographers and artists." The one thing she would want people to know about her, she says, "Is that I am trying." See www.armchair-epublishing.com.

Karla's birthday is December 2. Her horoscope tells that she is highly creative, spontaneous, loves variety but keeps everything firmly grounded.

GAIL MACDONALD

Gail MacDonald was born in Camden, Arkansas. The family moved to California when she was five, living mostly in Southern California. She says she and her husband Pat "fled" Southern California to live a dream life on Orcas Island, and moved to Bellingham in 1992. She has a BA in Spanish from Western Washington University.

When she retired from teaching, Gail wanted to exercise her passion for music. She believes that playing music is good for everyone and learning should be fun. As a certified ukulele teacher through the James Hill Ukulele Initiative, Gail brought "Ukulele in the Classroom" and has instructed students from beginning to ensemble level. Students learn musical literacy, to understand music better, learn about rhythm, keeping time and playing harmonies. Beginning classes run twelve weeks, covering note reading, ear training, music theory, strumming, harmony, singing and ensemble playing.

She says the ukulele is a versatile, portable and affordable instrument and … it's fun! Gail is the Director of BUG Ensemble (BUG-e) and co-leader of BUG. The Bellingham Ukulele Ensemble, with seventeen participants, plays in various venues around the area. Her dream is to continue developing the ensemble.

Gail and Pat have traveled extensively since 1991 and they will continue to see the world for as long as they can. At home, she enjoys quilting and reading books about and by authors from South America. She has a daughter, Maria, and a grandson, Patrick.

Asked what advice she would give to young women today, she says it would be simply, "Love your work." She is inspired by the challenges she faces and by the exceptional people around her. Surprisingly, she says she was very shy in high school. See www.bellinghamukulelegroup.com.

Gail's birthday is July 28. Her horoscope describes her as a warm and magnetic person, creative and talented at bringing harmony to the world around her. She is determined and organized with a strong sense of responsibility.

DEBORAH MCFARLANE

Deborah McFarlane, or Wine Diva Deb as she is known, escorts small groups of people on tours with a twist of wine. She says, "Wine Diva Deb was created after many years of searching for my passion – TRAVELING and WINE. Often we are traveling on a spacious 55-foot catamaran sailboat in Thailand or 50 foot plus sailboats in Greece where you will experience pleasures and adventure unavailable to larger vessels. As the name Wine Diva Deb implies, there is always an element of wine attached to each trip. In Greece, we visit a wonderful winery on the Island of Samos and a Greek wine festival on the Island of Lipsi, full of traditional dancing and drinking till dawn with the locals."

Many of Wine Diva Deb's trips are also onboard cruise ships. She says, "Being part of the group allows for special treatment, like personalized wine lunches and wine tastings onboard. We can visit ports near wine areas and have exclusive excursions just for our group. This is where you get to enjoy the comforts of a cruise ship with the intimacy of a Wine Diva Deb group."

Deb says, "I have always been a traveler, traveling all over the world to places like Greece, Turkey, Seychelles, England, Ireland, Germany, Tonga, Thailand, Costa Rica, Malaysia, Burma, just to name a few places. I have also loved everything about wine, how it is grown, cultivated, and then created into the lovely nectar of wine. Drinking wine in the place it was grown along with eating the food of the region is the most blissful experience I can imagine."

Growing up in San Jose, California, her first language was sign language...both her parents were deaf. She attended Humboldt University and graduated in Geology. Moving to Seattle in 1986, she worked at Fredrick & Nelson folding clothes in the Men's Department during the Christmas rush. In 1987 she got a job at Microsoft as a switchboard operator at $6 an hour and worked her way up to OEM account manager for IBM. She left Microsoft in 2000 and spent the next five years traveling.

Back in Seattle in 2005, she went back to school to study all things wine. She completed a two-year certificate in Sales and Marketing, Wine Technology, Graduating with Honors from the Wine Academy at South Seattle Community College, June 2006. She completed courses in: Enology, Viticulture, Sensory Evaluation, Food and Wine Pairing, Wines of Washington, Wine Marketing. History of Wine, Wines of the World. Advanced Food and Wine Pairing.

With the formation of Wine Diva Deb, LLC, Deb turned her passion for travel and wine into exciting new travel opportunities. She created her business to combine both her passions and share it with others. She asks, "Do you have an affinity for the finer things in life including wine and travel or know someone that does? Imagine sailing on the tranquil turquoise waters of the Mediterranean or the exotic Seas of Thailand, with pearly white beaches fringed by coconut palm trees, tropical islands covered in primary forest, clear waters which are outstanding for diving and snorkeling, or visiting famous wine regions of France like Châteauneuf-du-Pape, or cruising on a luxury cruise ship visiting wonderful ports in Spain, France, Italy or even Croatia."

A tribute from a past traveler in Greece tells us, "I experienced a totally relaxing time during my recent Greece adventure. Our skipper had in-depth knowledge of the Dodecanese islands, local customs, and scenic landmarks. She's an accomplished sailor and the boat was well provisioned. Our large group of strangers at the on-set blended into a homogenized clan that just kept on finding new ways to have a heap of fun...truly loved this experience!"

Deb is community-minded and believes in the power of networking. She belonged to the Woodinville Women & Wine, acting as their Official Travel Diva. She is a Volunteer for Wine Ambassadors and for Blue Ribbon Cooking School. Asked about advice for young women today, here is what she tells us:

"My one advice would be if you have a dream or a goal not to give up. For example I really wanted a job at Microsoft. I did not know how I was going to get that job but I started applying for every job I thought I could do. I had a Geology degree not computer science degree, but I did know a bit about computers. I applied for more than ten jobs over a year and finally got a job as a switchboard operator. Of course this is not what I really wanted to be doing at Microsoft but I got my foot in the door. After nine months of doing that and knowing everybody's phone number at Microsoft (at the time there were only 3,000 employees), I moved into Applications and became a marketing specialist, creating special reports for Mike Maples the VP of Applications, and worked on Bill Gates' PowerPoint slides. I started at pretty much the lowest job possible and just never gave up."

"Even in my Wine travel business when I get discouraged because I just cannot seem to fill a trip, I just keep thinking of ideas on how to reach people to share my passion for travel. I do love wine and the culture around wine in the world, which is what I have focused on, but sometimes it is a struggle to get people to join my trips. I often set a goal in my head: 'Okay, I would like 10 people to go to Iceland with me.' I keep that vision and mention it to people on a regular basis hoping to hit my goal. Sometimes I have 32 in my group which is about my max."

"I never know what kind of response I will get to a trip I put out there but I keep trying different things. Besides the European wine countries, my new adventure is a trip to Iceland, a cooking class and shopping trip to Mexico. I'm planning a trip to Russia and a fantastic Christmas River Cruise down the Danube." See www.winedivadeb.com.

Deb has a February 5 birthday. Her astrology chart indicates that she enjoys surprising people but can remain an enigma to the people around her. She is accommodating and kind with a strong intuitive instinct. She follows her own instincts and remains true to her heart.

MARY MICHAELSON

Mary Michaelson, now retired and living in Birch Bay, is enjoying an exciting new career… a Jazz singer with her band, Travelin' Light. They play for local private parties as well as senior centers. Also, she has found a Charming Gentleman and says she feels like life has started all over again.

Mary began her business life as a paralegal in Southern California. After moving to the Northwest, she became fascinated with the story of Phoebe Judson. Her innovative research revealed many surprising facts about this remarkable woman. Mary is the sole proprietor of "Aunt Phoebe's Corner," a company that conducts historical research about Judson and other pioneers in the Pacific Northwest, as well as other, related subjects. Mary is the editor/author of "Memory Book: Friends of Aunt Phoebe Reunion," published in 2006 by the Lynden Pioneer Museum where she was the Assistant Curator for six years.

Phoebe Goodell Judson (1831-1926) was an American pioneer and author. The Judsons left for the Washington Territory in March of 1853. Because of the large role she played during the 1870s through 1890s in the development of the Nooksack Valley (including giving Lynden its name), she is often referred to as the "Mother of Lynden." In 1886 she started the Northwest Normal School, which would become Western Washington University.

Mary was president of the Whatcom Writers and Publishers organization for several years, bringing fresh enthusiasm and growth to the group. Her newsletter for the group was especially popular, with articles contributed by the members as well as her own items and art work. The newsletter was sent out by email to writers throughout the community. Mary is continuing her research into the life of Phoebe Judson. She appears at corporate conferences, seminars, and museums with her PowerPoint presentation of Phoebe Judson and other Northwest Pioneers.

Mary is currently working on her own memoir with stories of growing up in Southern California. She has also resumed her artistic interests, joining The Tuesday Art Group, which meets, of course, every Tuesday from 10:00 a.m. to 4:00 p.m. Members take turns hosting the group. Each member does her own thing, from oils to watercolors, and even needlework. Mary is working on watercolor pencil drawings.

"Take care of your health," Mary advises young women. "Good health is the most important aspect for a good life." Her own daughter received brain damage in an automobile accident when she was just an infant and still requires supervised care.

Mary's birthday is June 28. Her horoscope chart shows that, while she does need her personal space, she comes alive and finds herself as an individual more readily when she is in a partnership situation.

TERRY RAY

Teresa M. "Terry" Ray served as the 2012-2014 President of the Washington State Business and Professional Women (BPW/WA), an organization with roots that go back to World War I, when the YWCA was asked to organize women's clubs across the country to help with the war effort.

After the war many of the women's clubs wanted to continue their nationwide affiliations. BPW/USA, founded in 1919, soon created state and local organizations with a mission of helping women succeed in the workplace. BPW still provides personal development programs, workshops, networking, and mentoring to help women realize their goals. One of the BPW mottos is: Women Helping Women. Monthly meetings, special events, and community projects encourage members to expand and exercise their leadership skills. Terry has been a part of BPW for some fifteen years, has chaired committees both in her local Everett BPW club and on the state level, and she's served as her local organizaton President. An energetic person with strong connections in the business community, Terry believes in cooperative networking, is happy to give help where she can and knows how to ask for and accept help when she needs it herself. A Washington state native, Terry has lived in the Seattle/Everett area for thirty-plus years. She is creative and artistic as well as practical; her business life is organized and efficient while her personal life is spontaneous and open to adventure.

In high school, where her main interest was drama, she took bookkeeping classes at her parent's insistence. "You must have practical skills to fall back on," they told her. With a degree in Industrial Education, her first job after college was working as Shop Teacher at Rainier Junior High. Since her name was Terry, people expected to see a man and were sometimes shocked to see a woman, especially a petite, cute, platinum blond woman… one who could and did work evenings as an Exotic Dancer and Go-Go Girl when she needed extra money.

Terry sang and danced in the chorus of CLO for about three years. She also sang at piano bars around Seattle, including the Edgewater Inn and The Canlis. "A soprano," she says, "I did vocal training with one of Barbara Streisand's voice coaches – Master David Kyle. I also trained with Freddie Colemank Founding Conductor and Artistic Director of the Seattle Choral Company."

Terry was also a seamstress. She worked in costuming for Civic Light Opera, and still sews for fun. She says, "I made Tiffany's prom dresses, and created my first motorcycle jacket out of a full deer hide with a Native American pattern from the leather store."

After working in accounting for eight years with King County, she took the IRS certification, deciding to become her own boss. She started her Freetrac Forensic Accounting business. She treats her clients' books and tax returns as if they were her own. "In accounting," she says, "the job isn't done until it is done right. There is no such thing as close enough." Deadlines and due dates don't intimidate Terry...she simply sees them as stimulants that fire her up. Regarding tax returns, she says, "Pay what you owe, but remember, you only have to pay Caesar his due." This past year, when she finally decided to retire, her clients simply wouldn't let her go...so she is now among the "semi-retired" professionals, working a couple of days a week, still serving those longtime core clients. And she does not have to commute; she works at home, in her long established, practical, home office.

Asked what advice she would give to young women today, Terry, always confident and optimistic, says, "Go for it! Don't be afraid to try something new, and learn as you go. Work hard, be creative, be open to change, and, above all, keep your sense of humor." Asked what's ahead for her in her "semi-retirement," she simply says "Who knows? No matter what you plan for or think you will do, life always has twists and turns and surprises."

When asked what about her would surprise people, she tells the story of being called into the principal's office (second grade), and told that she was accused of beating up a classmate. The principal looked her over, this tiny girl, and said, "You're Terry? I thought Terry was a boy. Well, tell me what happened." Terry explained, "He took my ball and wouldn't give it back. So I hit him." Principal, wide-eyed, "You beat up Billy the Bully?! Oh, just get out of here." See www.bpwwa.org.

Terry's birthday is January 17. According to an astrology description, people born on that date are career-oriented, often begin to plan professional goals when they are children, and have considerable ability to handle financial affairs.

IRENE ROBERTS

Irene Roberts is a Rep for Jusuru International, "A company," she says, "that has a product that gets rid of pain, inflammation, and wrinkles. After being rear ended, I developed migraine headaches, sciatic pain, and Fibroymalgia." At a meeting of the Bellevue Chamber of Commerce, Irene says, "I met a lady who showed me her monthly check of $25,000+, working with Scientist. I joined the company. Since 1989 I have been representing Scientist in the Preventive and Alternative Medicine. In 1999, Dr. Jesse Stoff invented a product that seeks and destroys Virus and Cancer cells. He saved my life from Ovarian, Lymph and Breast. Thanks to Jusuru I am pain FREE and looking for people who want to help me in my Mission, helping those who are suffering." Besides the sales commissions and the health benefits to herself, Irene works hard to win a Mercedes or a trip the Dominican Republic.

Irene comes from a family of twelve: seven girls and five boys. She is fourth child and first born daughter. Her father's dad was Spanish, his mother German and Italian. Her mother's parents were French and Spanish. Irene says, "My father believed we could do anything we put our minds to. He never allows us to say, I can't. We learned hard work, respect, honesty, and belief in ourselves."

Her father told his children that anytime someone offered a free class, make sure to take time and attend. "The more you learn, the more you will be able to achieve your dreams. Be a volunteer," he said. "You will be taught for free how to do a job."

Irene attended Cosmetology school, learning to sell Dorothy Gray products. She took modeling classes and modeled for Montgomery Ward. From Albuquerque, she went to Alaska when she was twenty-one years of age, and attended the University of Alaska, Juneau. She worked for the State of Alaska, Department of Corrections and was promoted to the Fiscal Department of Health and Social Services, paying medical bills, working on budgets, and helping with payroll.

Her dream was to work with the airline and she was admitted to be a flight attendant for TWA. But, she says, "I got married instead!" Her neighbor in Alaska was a manager for Wien Airlines and his wife became Irene's best friend. When Irene told them about her dreams, she was hired by Wien Airlines as a Ticket and Reservations Agent. Always an overachiever, she soon was selling the most tours in the whole company in Alaska and was made District Sales Manager. She became the first woman in the State to be in sales. She earned a trip around the world for being the first woman in sales for an airline with Lufthansa Airlines and PANAM.

After five years, Irene left her favorite job. She was expecting a child but lost it at five months. She tells us, "I got gangrene and died, but God did not want me, and I was sent back." For a year she suffered with low energy and was unable to work full time. She did work half days managing Avis Rent a Car for a month, Secretary to the Superintendent of Schools, and other short term jobs. She eventually returned to work for the State of Alaska, and became Executive for the Commissioner of DHSS. Two years later she was asked by Sheffield Hotels to work for them. She says, "They offered me so much I had to tell the Commissioner. He gave me his Blessings."

Within two years, with her exceptionally high sales, the hotel was out of the RED and in the BLACK. She was given $500 a month raise and promoted to SE Regional Sales Manager for eighteen hotels. She had made Alaska history again, as the first woman in sales for a hotel and the first for Sheffield. The owner of the hotel became Governor of the State of Alaska and Irene was paid to travel throughout the State introducing him.

After working twelve years with the hotel chain, Irene's husband moved to Washington state to open a log home business. Since she couldn't find a job that paid her what she had earned in Alaska, she helped her husband in his business

.

Irene first joined Business & Professional Women (BPW) in Alaska, gaining recognition as the Young Careerist and serving as Treasurer of the organization. She continued her BPW membership when she moved to Washington. She has served on various committees at the local, regional, and state levels, and BPW/WA State President 2002-2003. She is known as a highly enthusiastic and creative networking guru.

An active Volunteer, Irene is a past Park Board Commissioner for the City of Bellevue, the Current Ambassador for Bellevue Chamber of Commerce, Volunteer Bellevue Probation Officer,

Bellevue Youth Theatre Liaison Board Member, and Renton Chamber member. DeVry Advisory Board member and will begin mentoring to youth at Vision House, a place where they help the homeless. She also helps Beit Tikvahi, a non-profit helping the homeless in downtown Seattle, giving them blankets, scarfs, and jackets.

She loves to work in her flower garden, and loves to ski, but did not get there this year, she says. She loves reading the Bible, learning Prophecy. For television viewing, she chooses programs such as NCIS, NCIS LA, Shark Tank, and Criminal Minds.

Her advice to young women today would be to take advantage of opportunities to learn, work hard, help others, and let others help you. See www.jusuru.com/irene-sterling.

Irene's birthday is March 30. Her horoscope indicates that she is outgoing and assertive, yet mindful of others, sensitive, thoughtful, and very protective of those she loves. She may sometimes require time to herself to recharge her emotional batteries.

LISA STONE

Lisa Stone's advice to young women today is, "Be outraged! We still don't have equality, by far!" Lisa is the Executive Director of Legal Voice in Seattle, an organization that works to ensure justice for women, girls, and sexual minorities, with three key strategies: litigation, legislative and policy advocacy, and legal education of individuals and communities. They work with the "Legal Voice Women's Bill of Rights."

Legal Voice believes that women – all women – have these fundamental rights:
- The right to equal treatment and to be free from discrimination
- The right to decide when and how to form and maintain their families
- The right to be safe wherever they are
- The right to economic equality and independence
- The right to be healthy and active

Having worked as a retail manager, a lawyer for the government and in private practice, and as an environmental manager for an oil-spill cleanup company, it wasn't until she became the Executive Director of Legal Voice that Lisa says she found the place she belongs. In1988 her casual inquiry about volunteering for the organization led to a three-year case representing clinics, patients, and doctors against anti-choice extremists blocking medical facilities. She was hooked on the cause and the people of Legal Voice and continued as a volunteer for several more years until she finagled a paying job as Executive Director in 1995.

Lisa's work at Legal Voice can be summed up by the sign she carried at the 2004 March for Women's Lives, which featured a photo of her late mother at the 1992 March: its caption read, "No going back . . . I promised my mother." She says working at Legal Voice permits her to speak her mind about women's rights. Lisa oversees the work of both staff and volunteers, organizes fund raising events, and speaks at every opportunity to other groups around the state. See www.legalvoice.org.

After attending California State University, Fresno, Lisa chose the University of Washington for law school. She says she moved to Seattle for the rain. Coming from California, Lisa says she experienced a bit of "geography discrimination" . . . until she pointed out that her dad was born in Sequim. That made her practically a native Washingtonian. She lives in the Capitol Hill District and loves the metropolitan life. In her leisure time she enjoys theater, white water canoeing, and the Mariners. She loves murder mysteries, something she says she inherited from both her mother and her grandmother. She also loves Disneyland and says it really is the happiest place on earth! Both she and her husband are looking forward to early retirement within the next few years. They love travel and exploring and plan to do a lot more of it.

Lisa's birthday is December 19. Her horoscope chart describes her as a magnetic person with a flair for the dramatic. She has exceptional creative powers, is gentle and patient, but also very determined: a person who puts her heart into whatever she does.

DIANE TURNER

Diane Turner is owner, editor, and publisher of the Northwest Retirement Magazine, both in print and online. The magazine appeals to a new generation of the over-fifty community with articles that take an up-to-date look at retirement, work, leisure, financial planning, and health care.

With a readership of over 10,000 in Whatcom County, Washington, it also provides its advertisers with an opportunity to reach this important demographic with information, services, and products. Articles feature local residents, local businesses, and local events.

In addition managing this magazine, Diane is also a successful realtor in Henderson, Nevada, where she has lived for the past few years. She has had a varied and fulfilling career history. With a BA in Communication and an MA in Organizational Leadership, Diane began her career as a high school English teacher. She spent over ten years as Director of Business Development and Marketing for hospital corporations in California. She also directed children's theatre for a private non-profit organization in Newport Beach, California.

In 1992, she worked as a successful realtor in Portland, Oregon where she was third in an office of forty agents for selling properties. Her major source of new clients came through her weekly Buyers Seminars.

In Bellingham, she started a new events department for the Port of Bellingham, hired and trained a staff to handle major events, business meetings and community group meetings. Together with a group of Latino businesses, Diane established The Washington Latino Business Association. With fifty members, they met monthly to promote local business and give scholarships to aspiring high school students in the area. In 2003, she published her first novel, The Promesa Strategy, a political thriller.

In a message to young women today, Diane says, "I still work hard in Real Estate, publishing and writing. In my free time I travel, sew, read, teach Sunday school and jog every morning. I would tell young women to have passion for life and to not be afraid to grab opportunities when they arise." See www. nwretirementmag.com.

Diane birthday is January 27. Her horoscope chart indicates that she places high value on her personal freedom. She has a creative style and an analytical mind. She is an excellent teacher and good at encouraging and motivating people.

MIKELANN VALTERRA

Mikelann Valterra's advice to women is: Demand what you are really worth, learn how to ask (negotiate) for more. "Too often," she says, "women underestimate the value of their services and end up earning much less than they could and should." She also advises, "Track what you spend and watch out for emotional buttons."

Mikelann is an author, speaker and leader in the field of personal finance. Her passion is to help professionals escape the money fog, feel more in control of their finances, and love their financial life. She believes everyone can truly heal and transform their relationship to money. And she is a money coach/ Financial Recovery Coach, addressing practical money matters as well as the emotional components that can lead to unhealthy financial behaviors.

The author of *Why Women Earn Less: How to make what you're really worth*, as well as multiple workbooks and audios, Mikelann has appeared on dozens of radio shows, television spots and in newspapers across the United States, as well as writing her own blog.

Mikelann first studied economics and then earned her masters degree in Consciousness Studies and Psychology. She then earned her certification as a Financial Recovery Counselor and Coach. In her seminars combining psychology, personal finance and brain science, Mikelann transforms the attendee's relationship to money. She emphasizes that stress over mounting financial burdens, debt and out-of-control expenses in their lives can lead to chronic anxiety, impacting relationships both in and out of the work place. Health and well-being are compromised, and people feel depleted. By helping the audience to understand how their brains and their unconscious beliefs about money lead them to spend in ways they do not realize, she demystifies why we really do what we do when it comes to money.

"We all have personal 'money stories' that were programmed into us at early ages," Mikelann says, "stories that came from our first experiences of witnessing how money was handled around us. In fact, our internal landscape is ripe with hidden money meanings and emotional spending triggers. On top of this, we often spend because it feels good, or to make ourselves feel better. Spending money can actually release 'feel good' neurochemicals in the healthy brain."

"I work with many amazing people on their relationship to money. Often times, my clients feel as if money is their 'final frontier'— while they've done work on many areas of their lives, money remains frustrating and confusing. I work one-on-one with clients, mentoring them and teaching them the skills needed to gain control over their money. While supplying the tools needed for effective money management, I also help my clients address the underlying issues that help shape, and may continue to fuel, their unhealthy money behaviors.

My goal is to help my clients feel more in control of money and have more peace and less stress around their finances."

"Besides my private practice which focuses on working with professional women on their relationship to money, I spend my professional time working on MoneyMinderOnline--growing the user base for MoneyMinder: marketing, software development and creating content for women in the form of articles and podcasts etc." MoneyMinderOnline is a tool designed to help a person develop a lasting healthy relationship to money and experience flexible, guilt-free spending. MoneyMinder is a financial tracking and spending plan software designed by women for women. "It gives you the awareness, information, and savvy you need to track where your money is going for monthly and yearly expenses. It even predicts where you'll be financially at month's end… or the end of the year."

Not only was Mikelann born and raised in the Northwest, and attended Western Washington University, she still lives within a few blocks of her parents' house in the same Seattle neighborhood where she was raised. As to hobbies, she has several. She says, "I adore keeping up with my zany teenage son. I am very involved in his high school athletics programs. I personally enjoy watching the NFL as well. Following the Seattle Seahawks has been a hobby for many years. I love to read historical detective fiction, I adore science fiction, and I'm fortunate to have a lot of family and friends in the Seattle area. So there is plenty of time for evening dinners and weekend adventures." See www.seattlemoneycoach.com.

Mikelann was born on July 2. Her horoscope chart points out that she has great strength of character and a gift for seeing the value of things. She is a natural leader and understands that compromise can be important to success.

WOMEN GOVERNORS

The first three women governors of any American state replaced their husbands. Many later women governors have been elected in their own right or have succeeded an incumbent. Here's a list of the women governors in the United States, in chronological order:

Nellie Tayloe Ross:
Wyoming, Democrat, 1925-1927

Miriam "Ma" Ferguson:
Texas, Democrat, 1925-1927, 1933-1935

Lurleen Wallace:
Alabama, Democrat, 1967-1968

Ella Grasso:
Connecticut, Democrat, 1975-1980

Dixy Lee Ray:
Washington, Democrat, 1977-1981

Vesta Roy:
New Hampshire, Republican, 1982-1983

Martha Layne Collins:
Kentucky, Democrat, 1984-1987

Madeleine Kunin:
Vermont, Democrat, 1985-1991

Kay Orr:
Nebraska, Republican, 1987-1991

Rose Mofford:
Arizona, Democrat, 1988-1991

Joan Finney:
Kansas, Democrat, 1991-1995

Ann Richards:
Texas, Democrat, 1991-1995

Barbara Roberts:
Oregon, Democrat, 1991-1995

Christine Todd Whitman:
New Jersey, Republican, 1994-2001

Jane Dee Hull:
Arizona, Republican, 1997-2003

Jeanne Shaheen:
New Hampshire, Democrat, 1997-2003

Nancy Hollister:
Ohio, Republican, 1998-1999

Jane Swift:
Massachusetts, Republican, 2001-2003

Judy Martz:
Montana, Republican, 2001-2005

Sila Maria Calderon:
Puerto Rico, Popular Democratic Party, 2001-2005

Ruth Ann Minner:
Delaware, Democrat, 2001-2009

Linda Lingle:
Hawaii, Republican, 2002-2010

Jennifer M. Granholm:
Michigan, Democrat, 2003-2011

Janet Napolitano:
Arizona, Democrat, 2003-2009

Kathleen Sebelius:
Kansas, Democrat, 2003-2009

Oline Walker:
Utah, Republican, 2003-2005

Kathleen Blanco:
Louisiana, Democrat, 2004-2008

M. Jodi Rell:
Connecticut, Republican, 2004-2011

Christine Gregoire:
Washington, Democrat, 2004-2013

Sarah Palin:
Alaska, Republican, 2006-2009

Beverly Perdue:
North Carolina, Democrat, 2009-2013

Jan Brewer:
Arizona, Republican, 2009-

Susana Martinez:
New Mexico, Republican, 2011-

Mary Fallin:
Oklahoma, Republican, 2011-

Nikki Haley:
South Carolina, Republican, 2011-

Maggie Hassan:
New Hampshire, Democrat, 2013 –

THE GREAT NORTHWEST

Nicknamed Evergreen and roughly divided east/west by the Cascades, Washington has a population of around seven million, with half the residents living in the Seattle metropolitan area. The Northwest corner of Washington is home to a diverse population, small friendly towns, and both winter and summer sports areas. Washington's marine highway has a fleet of 28 ferries navigating Puget Sound and its inland waterways to 20 different ports, with almost 150,000 sailings each year. Olympia, about 60 miles southwest of Seattle, is the state capital, the county seat of Thurston County, and the home of Evergreen State College.

Seattle, the largest city in the Pacific Northwest, is proudly known as "a city of neighborhoods," with each neighborhood maintaining a distinctive style and flavor. Here are just a few of those neighborhoods:

Ballard is a neighborhood in the northwestern part of Seattle, and historically the traditional center of Seattle's Scandinavian seafaring community who were drawn to the area because of the salmon fishing opportunities.

Capitol Hill neighborhood is a densely populated residential district and one of the city's most prominent nightlife and entertainment districts. With a rich and diverse history, Capitol Hill is highly regarded for its arts and culture.

Chinatown International District is known as the cultural hub for Pan-Asian Americans, with Chinese, Filipino, Japanese, Vietnamese and Southeast Asians living and working together. Highlights here include specialty gift shops, Asian restaurants and specialty markets.

Pike Place Market in downtown Seattle is one of the city's biggest draws, featuring fresh seafood, artisan chocolates, and the first Starbucks coffee shop in the Pacific Northwest.

Queen Anne is an oasis of stately homes and century-old trees, good food and culture, including Lower Queen Anne's wealth of theaters, opera, ballet and Seattle International Film Festival's year-round events, within walking distance of downtown.

A few typical towns in the Northwest corner of Washington include:

Anacortes is a town of friendly neighbors and low crime rate. The Anacortes Arts Festival in August draws 80,000 visitors over a busy weekend. Located on Fidalgo Island, Anacortes is roughly halfway between Seattle and Vancouver, BC. The climate is mild, with annual rainfall of 26", daytime temperatures averaging in the 40s during the winter, 70s in the summer, and a few inches of snowfall each winter.

Bellingham, the county seat of Whatcom County and home of Western Washington University, is the twelfth-largest city in the state. The boundaries of the city encompass the former towns of Fairhaven, Whatcom, Sehome, and Bellingham. Driving time to either Seattle or Vancouver BC is approximately an hour and a half from Bellingham.

Birch Bay is a family friendly town approximately 100 miles north of Seattle, 35 miles south of Vancouver, BC, and just 7 miles from the Canadian border. The half-moon shaped bay, with a large tide flat of sand several square miles in size, is considered perfect for clamming, building sand sculptures, flying kites, wake boarding, and windsurfing.

Duvall, named after James Duvall, a logger who homesteaded there is 1871, is approximately 25 miles northeast of Seattle. The Snoqualmie Valley Trail is a 30-plus mile regional trail that meanders along the Snoqualmie River from Duvall to North Bend.

Everett, approximately 25 miles north of Seattle, is the western terminus of U.S. Route 2. With a population just over 100,000, it is the county seat of and the largest city in Snohomish County. Everett has more than 1,600 acres of parks, trails and playgrounds, nearly 50 miles of freshwater and saltwater shorelines and the largest public marina on the west coast.

Renton is about eleven miles southeast of downtown Seattle located on the southeast shore of Lake Washington. Renton's early economy was based on coal mining, clay production, and timber export. Today, Renton is best known as the final assembly of Boeing commercial airplanes.

Woodinville, part of the Seattle metropolitan area, has waterfront parks on the Sammamish River, extensive winery and brewery grounds, and densely wooded residential areas. There is also a large population with Woodinville mailing addresses in adjacent unincorporated areas of King and Snohomish counties. Also noteworthy of the area is the elegant Willows Lodge and the Herb Farm restaurant.

NW Images by Tony Locke Photography

NW Images by Tony Locke Photography

NW Images by Tony Locke Photography

NW Images by Tony Locke Photography

Networking Connections

In every community, innumerable groups offer opportunities for professional, civic, and social networking, career advancement, personal and professional growth. This list is just a small sampling.

Business and Professional Women (BPW/WA): active local organizations in the Seattle metropolitan area, promotes equity and economic self-sufficiency, as well as leadership development, for all working women with regular networking events.

Women On A Mission To Earn Commission (WOAMTEC): Goal is to build a positive networking atmosphere where seasoned professional business women can come together to share ideas, offer support, and create solid business alliances.

Chat with Women: Seattle-based radio show host of Chat with Women organize regular social events for local women who want to learn, grow, change their lives and have some fun along the way.

CRAVE Seattle: a community of women entrepreneurs and business owners who support and inspire each other to succeed. Women are invited to attend an event to see if CRAVE is right for them.

Girl Power Hour (GPH): a quarterly networking and professional development forum for young women in Seattle and the Eastside. GPH is known for its stylish cocktail events, with interests ranging from fashion to social media.

eWomenNetwork: serves as a hub where professional women can connect, network and support each other to grow their business, as well as to showcase their products and services.

Women of Wisdom (WOW): organizes local networking events and workshops for women interested in a holistic approach to the pursuit of their professional, business, personal, family and spiritual objectives.

Women's Professional Network (WPN): offers members free listing in the Member Directory, with links to their email and website, free display table in the WPN Business Center, free announcements in the printed monthly newsletter, on our website, or both

Toastmasters International: a nonprofit educational organization that operates clubs worldwide for the purpose of helping members improve their communication, public speaking and leadership skills.

SUGGESTED READING

Work With Me: The 8 Blind Spots Between Men and Women in Business, by Barbara Annis and John Gray. Barbara Annis and John Gray argue that men and women are biologically wired to think and react differently to situations, and have "gender blind spots" when it comes to understanding their co-workers' behavior.

A Rising Tide: Financing Strategies for Women-Owned Firms, by Susan Coleman and Alicia Robb. Susan Coleman and Alicia Robb point out that women sometimes want to keep their businesses small in order to balance their family responsibilities.

The XX factor: How Working Women are Creating a New Society, by Alison Wolf. Alison Wolf, the director of public policy and management at Kings College London, states that there are now around seventy million highly educated, high-earning women around the world and that these women have more in common with elite men than with other women.

Women, Work & The Art of Savoir Faire: Business Sense & Sensibility, by Mireille Guiliano. Mireille Guiliano offers practical advice to help women make the most of work without ever losing sight of what is most important: feeling good, facing challenges, getting ahead, and maximizing pleasure at every opportunity.

Lean In - Women, Work, and the Will to Lead. by Sheryl Sandberg. Sheryl Sandberg shares her personal stories, uses research to shine a light on gender differences, and offers practical advice to help women achieve their goals. The book challenges us to change the conversation from what women can't do to what we can do.

Where Have All The Smart Women Gone, by Alice Ann Rowe, Ph.D. Alice Rowe points out that women of intelligence often find themselves trapped in a Double Bind: striving to achieve professional success and still feeling societal pressure to assume more conventional roles.

42 Rules for Effective Connections, by Bonnie Ross-Parker and Cindy Elsberry.

Anne Alberg, contributor of Rule #12, advises: Actively listen to determine how you can contribute to others.

Why Women Earn Less: How to make what you're really worth, by Mikelann Valterra. Mikelann Valterra tells us, "Too often women underestimate the value of their services and end up earning much less than they could and should."

Wine Types: Discover Your Inner Grape, by Maureen Kelly. Maureen Kelly gives us a quote from Phillippe de Rothschild who says, "Excellent wine generates enthusiasm. And whatever you do with enthusiasm is generally successful."

ABOUT THE AUTHOR

Carolyn Leeper lives in Bellingham, Washington, with her husband Ed and Cora the Cat. Carolyn has enjoyed a widely varied business background: secretary, bookkeeper, direct sales, business school instructor, event planner, writer, editor, and twenty-five years as a travel counselor for both leisure and corporate clients. She is a member of the Whatcom Writers & Publishers (WWP), the Women's Professional Network (WPN) and a past state president of the Washington Business & Professional Women (BPW/WA). Carolyn believes that most women take a look at the stated requirements of a job and immediately begin overachieving... and loving it.

Made in the USA
San Bernardino, CA
18 April 2014